Life Changing Qutoes of Swami Vivekananda

Conceptualized and Designed By
Farhad Haque

© 2013 by Farhad Haque

All rights reserved. No part of this publication may be reproduced, distributed, or transmitted in any form or by any means, or stored in a database or retrival system, without the prior written permission of the publisher.

Designed By
Farhad Haque
FH Interactive Creations.

Feedback:
farhadhaquesu@gmail.com

ACKNOWLEDGEMENTS

I'd like to say thank you to:
Farida Yasmin, who makes everyday of my life a masterpiece;
Aminul Haque, my father;
Dilruba Akter, my wonderful sister;
Nazmus Sakib Rishan, new member of our family and amazon.com.

"Take up one idea. Make that one idea your life-think of it, live on that idea. Let the brain, muscles, nerves, every part of your body, be full of that idea, and just leave every other idea alone. This is the way to success."

SWAMI VIVEKANANDA

 FARHAD HAQUE

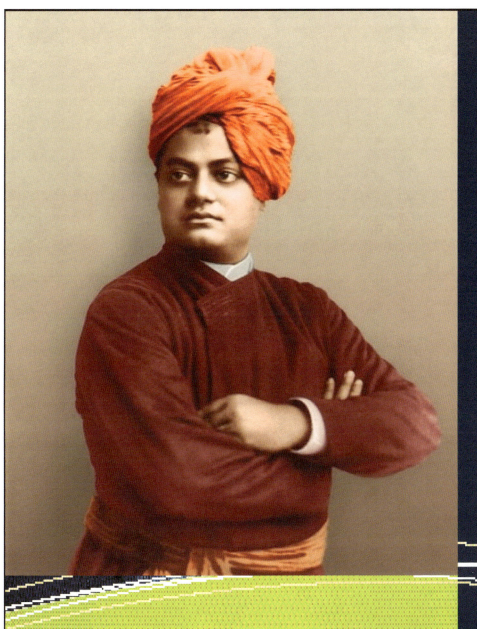

"All power is within you; you can do anything and everything. Believe in that, do not believe that you are weak; do not believe that you are half-crazy lunatics, as most of us do nowdays. You can do any thing and everything, without even the guidance of any one. Stand up and express the divinity within you."

SWAMI VIVEKANANDA

 FARHAD HAQUE

"Always discriminate….your body, your house, the people and the world are absolutely unreal like a dream. Always think that the body is only an inert instrument. And the Atman within is your real nature."

SWAMI VIVEKANANDA

 FARHAD HAQUE

"Understanding human nature is the highest knowledge, and only by knowing it can we know God? It is also a fact that the knowledge of God is the highest knowledge, and only by knowing God can we understand human nature."

SWAMI VIVEKANANDA

 FARHAD HAQUE

"Hold to the idea, "I am not the mind, I see that I am thinking, I am watching my mind act," and each day the identification of yourself with thoughts and feelings will grow less, untill at last you can entirely separate yourself from the mind and actually know it to be apart from yourself."

SWAMI VIVEKANANDA

 FARHAD HAQUE

"All knowledge that the world has never received comes from the mind; the infinite library of the universe is in our own mind."

SWAMI VIVEKANANDA

 FARHAD HAQUE

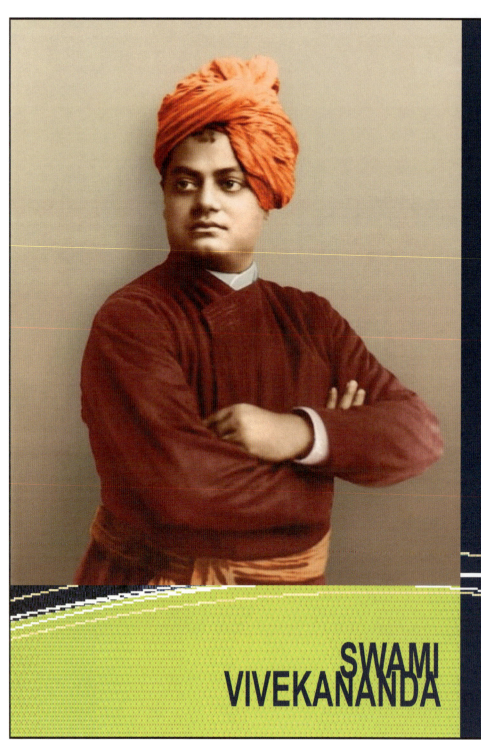

"If the mind is intensely eager, everything can be accomplished—mountains can be crumbled into atoms."

SWAMI VIVEKANANDA

 FARHAD HAQUE

"Don't look back-forward, infinite energy, infinite enthusiasm, infinite patience-then alone can great deeds be accomplished."

SWAMI VIVEKANANDA

FARHAD HAQUE

"Brave, bold people, these are what we want. What we want is vigor in the blood, strength in the nerves, iron muscles and nerves of steel, not satisfying namby-pamby ideas. Avoid all these. Avoid all mystery. There is no mystery in religion."

SWAMI VIVEKANANDA

 FARHAD HAQUE

"Be strong! Don't talk of ghosts and devils. We are the living devils. The sign of death is weakness. Whatever is weak, avoid! It is death. If it is strength, go down into hell and get hold of it! There is salvation only for the brave."

SWAMI VIVEKANANDA

 FARHAD HAQUE

"Be perfectly resigned, perfectly unconcerned; then alone can you do any true work. No eyes can see the real forces; we can only see the results. Put out self, forget it; just let God work, it is His business."

SWAMI VIVEKANANDA

 FARHAD HAQUE

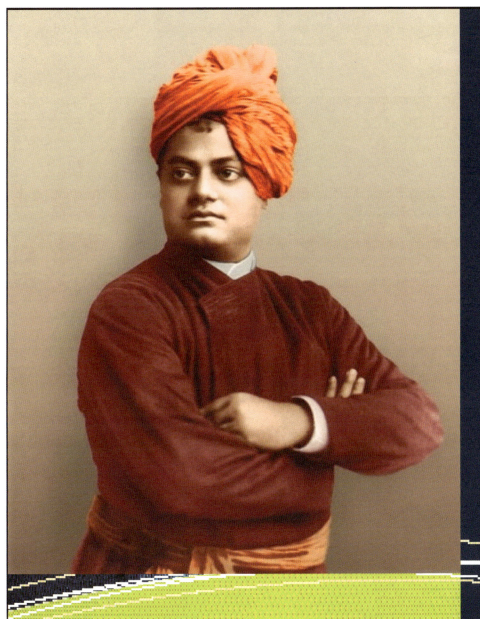

"Be brave! Be strong! Be fearless! Once you have taken up the spiritual life, fight as long as there is any life in you. Even though you know you are going to be killed, fight till you "are killed." Don't die of fright. Die fighting. Don't go down till you are knocked down."

SWAMI VIVEKANANDA

 FARHAD HAQUE

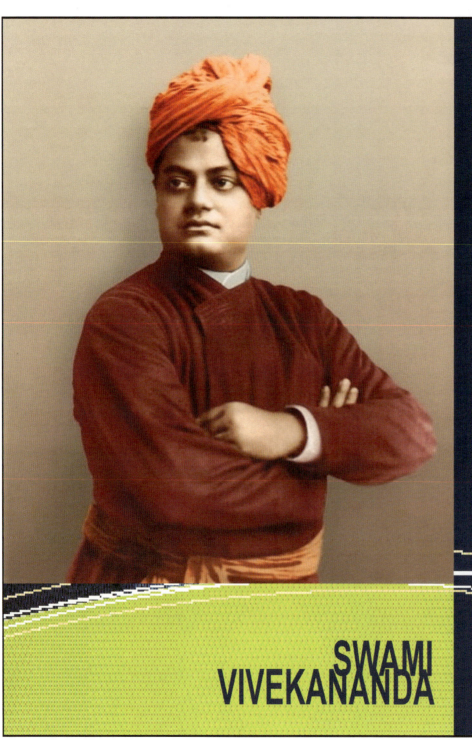

"Why are people so afraid? The answer is that they have made themselves helpless and dependent on others. We are so lazy, we do not want to do anything ourselves."

SWAMI VIVEKANANDA

 FARHAD HAQUE

"There is no help for you outside of yourself; you are the creator of the universe. Like the silkworm you have built a cocoon around yourself.....Burst your own cocoon and come out to the beautiful butterfly, as the free soul. Then alone you will see Truth."

SWAMI VIVEKANANDA

 FARHAD HAQUE

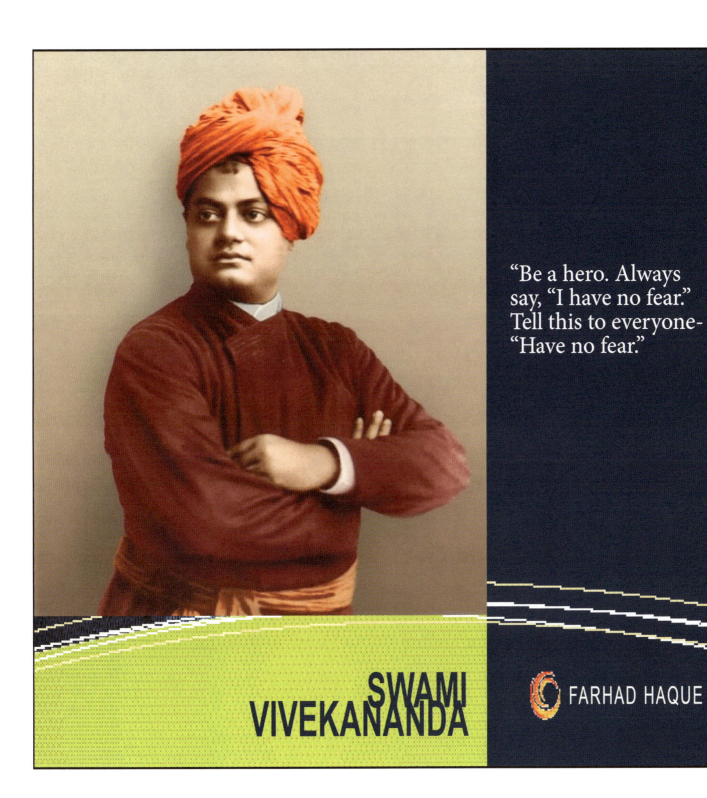

"Stand up, be bold, be strong. Take the whole responsibility on your own shoulders, and know that you are the creator of your own destiny. All the strength and success you want is within yourselves. Therefore, make your own future."

SWAMI VIVEKANANDA

 FARHAD HAQUE

"To succeed you must have tremendous perseverance, tremendous will. "I will drink the ocean," says the persering soul, "at my will mountains will crumble." Have that sort of energy, that sort of will, work hard, and you will reach the goal."

SWAMI VIVEKANANDA

 FARHAD HAQUE

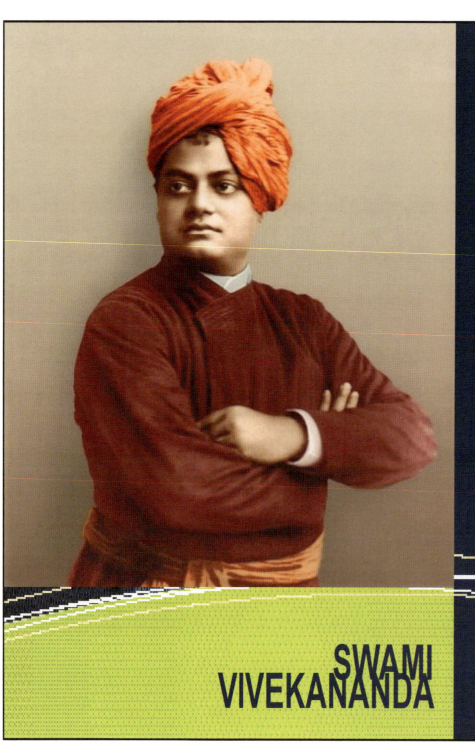

"Strength is life,
Weakness is Death.
Expansion is Life,
Contraction is Death.
Love is Life,
Hatred is Death."

SWAMI VIVEKANANDA

 FARHAD HAQUE

"When I Asked God for Strength
He Gave Me Difficult Situations to Face

When I Asked God for Brain and Brown
He Gave Me Puzzles in Life to Solve

When I Asked God for Happiness
He Showed Me Some Unhappy People

When I Asked God for Wealth
He Showed Me How to Work Hard

When I Asked God for Peace
He showed Me How to Help Others.

God Gave Me Nothing I Wanted

He Gave Me Everything I Needed."

SWAMI VIVEKANANDA

 FARHAD HAQUE

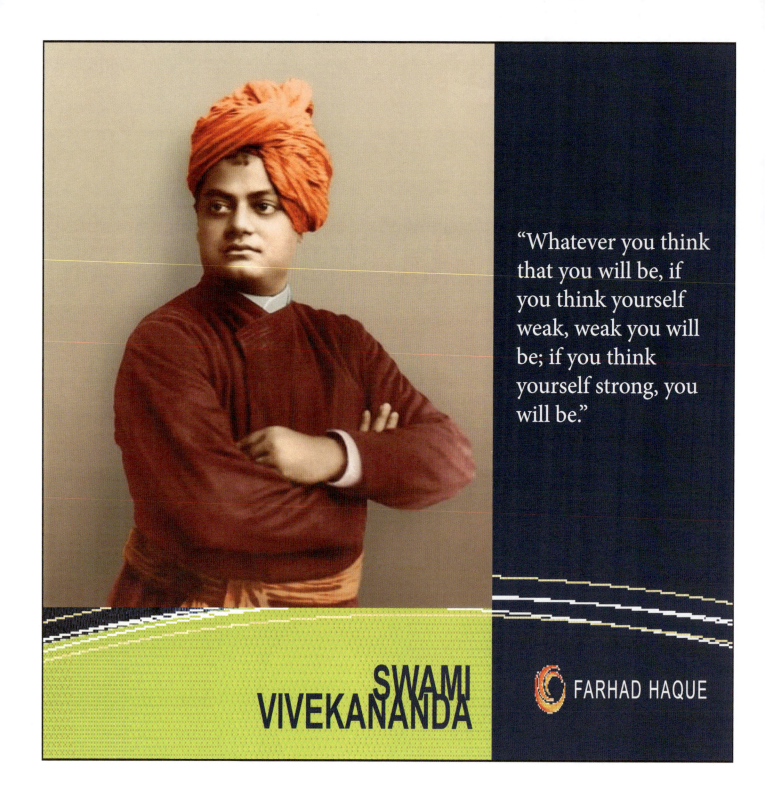

"A tremendous stream is flowing toward the ocean, carrying us all along with it; and though like straws and scraps of paper we may at times float aimlessly about, in the long run we are sure to join the Ocean of Life and Bliss."

SWAMI VIVEKANANDA

 FARHAD HAQUE

"I do not want to get material life. I do not want sense-life but something higher." That is renunciation. Then by the power of meditation undo the mischief that has been done.

SWAMI VIVEKANANDA

 FARHAD HAQUE

"Face the brutes. That is a lesson for all life-face the terrible, face it boldly. Like the monkeys, the hardships of life fall back when we cease to flee before them."

SWAMI VIVEKANANDA

 FARHAD HAQUE

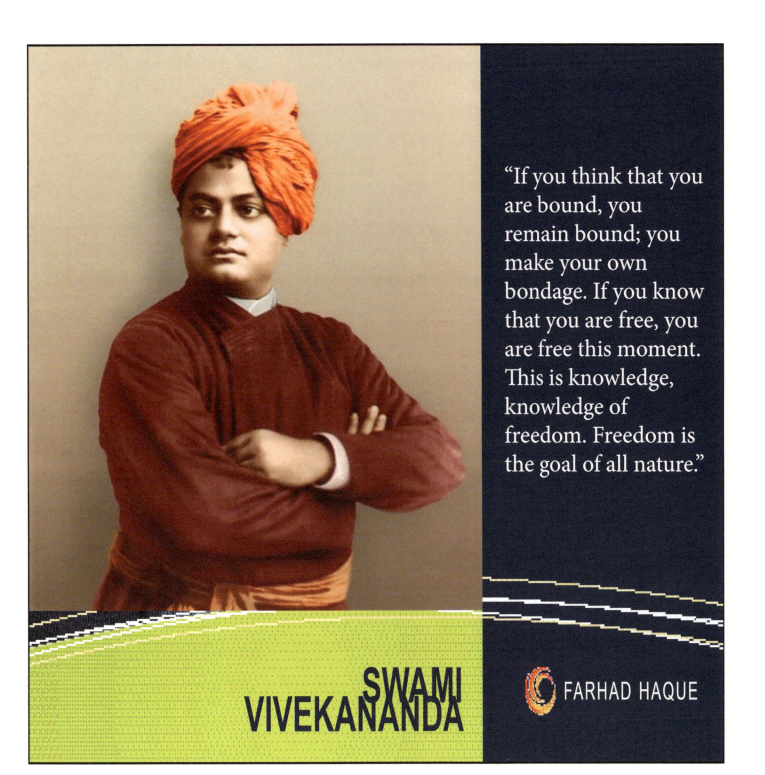

"Even the greatest fool can accomplish a task if it were after his or her heart. But the intelligent ones are those who can convert every work into one that suits their taste."

SWAMI VIVEKANANDA

 FARHAD HAQUE

"If you want to have life, you have to die every moment for it. Life and death are only different expressions of the same thing looked at from different standpoints; they are the falling and the rising of the same wave, and the two form one whole."

SWAMI VIVEKANANDA

 FARHAD HAQUE

"All love is expansion, all selfishness is contraction. Love is therefore the only law of life. He who loves lives, he who is selfish is dying. Therefore love for love's sake, because it is law of life, just as you breathe to live."

SWAMI VIVEKANANDA

FARHAD HAQUE

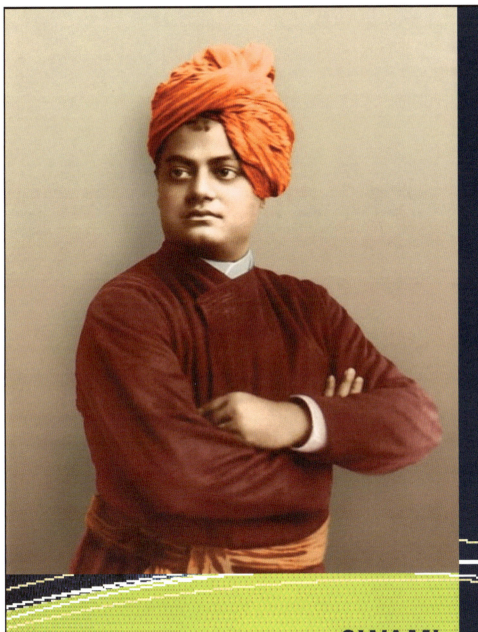

"After every happiness comes misery; they may be far apart or near. The more advanced the soul, the more quickly does one follow the other. What we want is neither happiness nor misery. Both make us forget our true nature; both are chains.. one iron, one gold, behind both is Atman, who knows neither happiness nor misery. These are states, and states must ever change; but the nature of the Atman is bliss, peace, unchanging. We have not to get it, we have it, only wash away the dross and see it."

SWAMI VIVEKANANDA

 FARHAD HAQUE

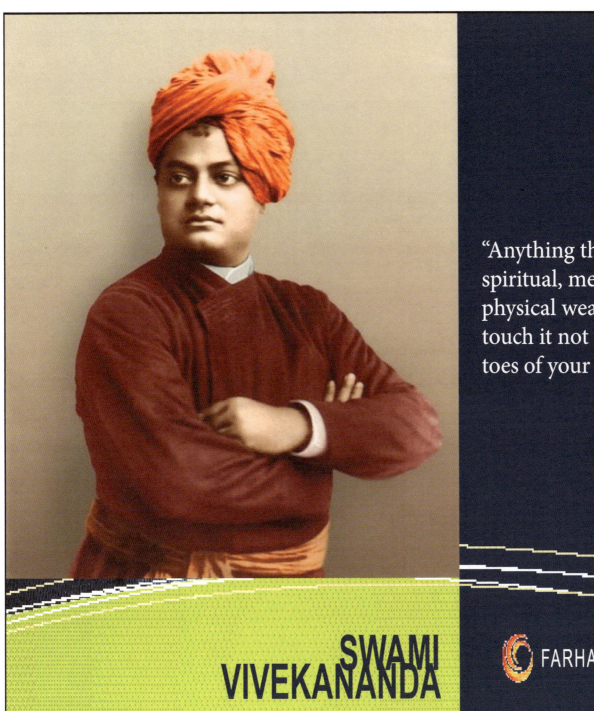

"Anything that brings spiritual, mental, or physical weakness, touch it not with the toes of your feet."

SWAMI VIVEKANANDA

FARHAD HAQUE

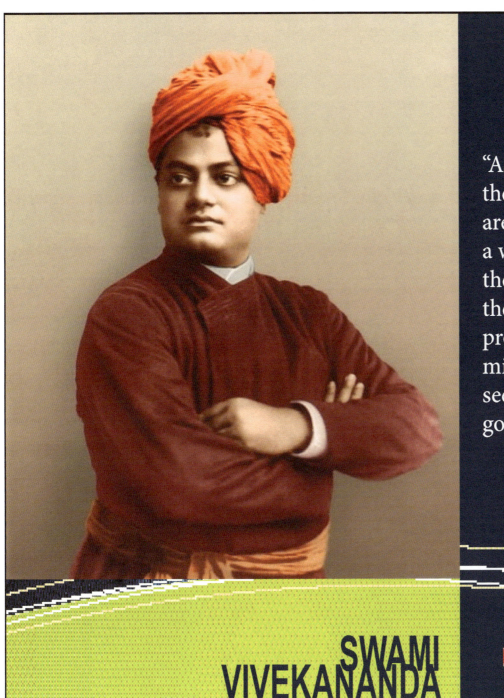

"Astrology and all these mystical things are generally signs of a weak mind; therefore as soon as they are becoming prominent in our minds, we should see a physician, take good food, and rest."

SWAMI VIVEKANANDA

 FARHAD HAQUE

"Avoid excessive merriment. A mind in that state never becomes calm; it becomes fickle. Excessive merriment will always be f ollowed by sorrow. Tears and laughter are near kin. People so often run from one extreme to the other."

SWAMI VIVEKANANDA

 FARHAD HAQUE

"All that is real in me is God; all that is real in God is I. The gulf between God and human beings is thus bridged. Thus we find how, by knowing God, we find the kingdom of heaven within us."

SWAMI VIVEKANANDA

 FARHAD HAQUE

"All truth is eternal. Truth is nobody's property; no race; no individual can lay any exclusive claim to it. Truth is the nature of all souls."

SWAMI VIVEKANANDA

FARHAD HAQUE

"All who have actually attained any real religious experience never wrangle over the form in which the different religions are expressed. They know that the soul of all religions is the same and so they have no quarrel with anybody just because he or she does not speak in the same tongue."

SWAMI VIVEKANANDA

 FARHAD HAQUE

"Whose meditation is real and effective? Who can really surrender to the will of God? Only the person whose mind has been purified by selfless work."

SWAMI VIVEKANANDA

 FARHAD HAQUE

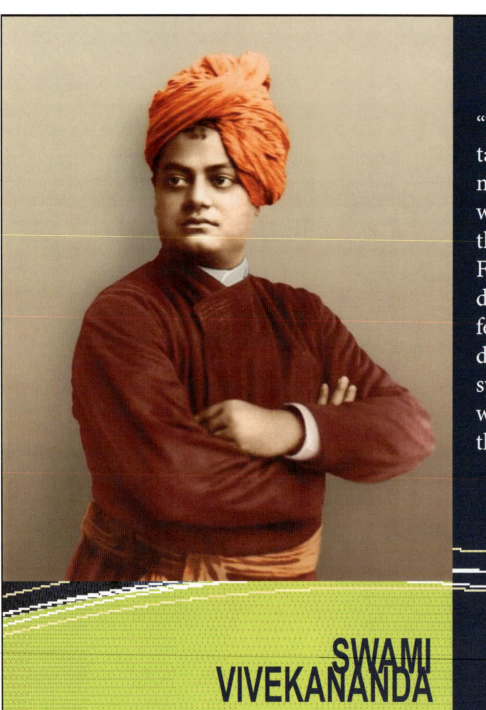

"What is the use of talking of one's mistakes to the world? They cannot thereby be undone. For what one has done one must suffer; one must try and do better. The world sympathizes only with the strong and the powerful."

SWAMI VIVEKANANDA

 FARHAD HAQUE

"We came to enjoy; we are being enjoyed. We came to rule; we are being ruled. We came to work; we are being worked. All the time, we find that. And this comes into every detail of our life."

SWAMI VIVEKANANDA

 FARHAD HAQUE

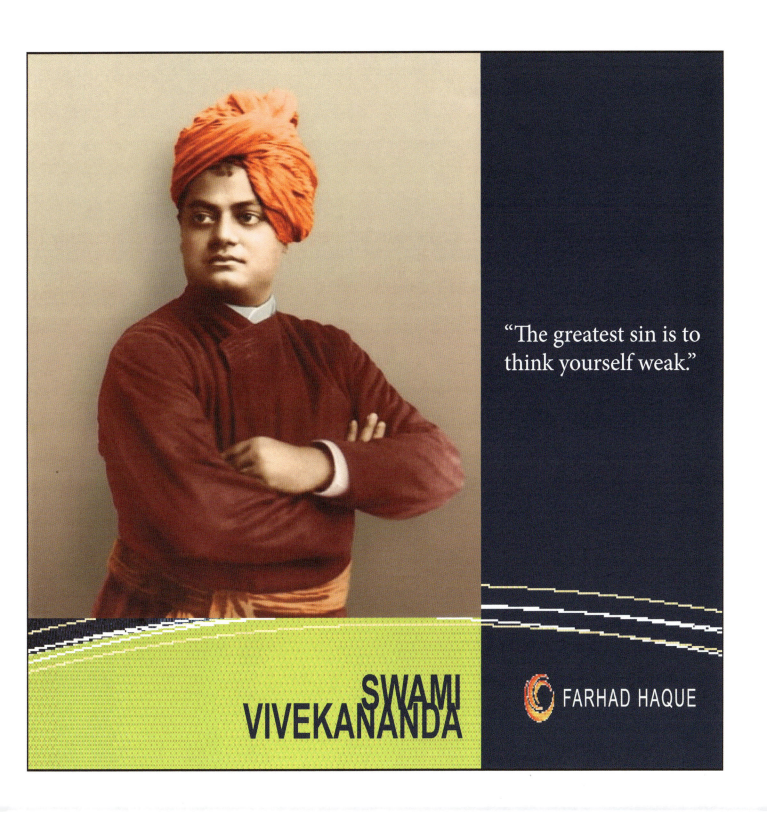

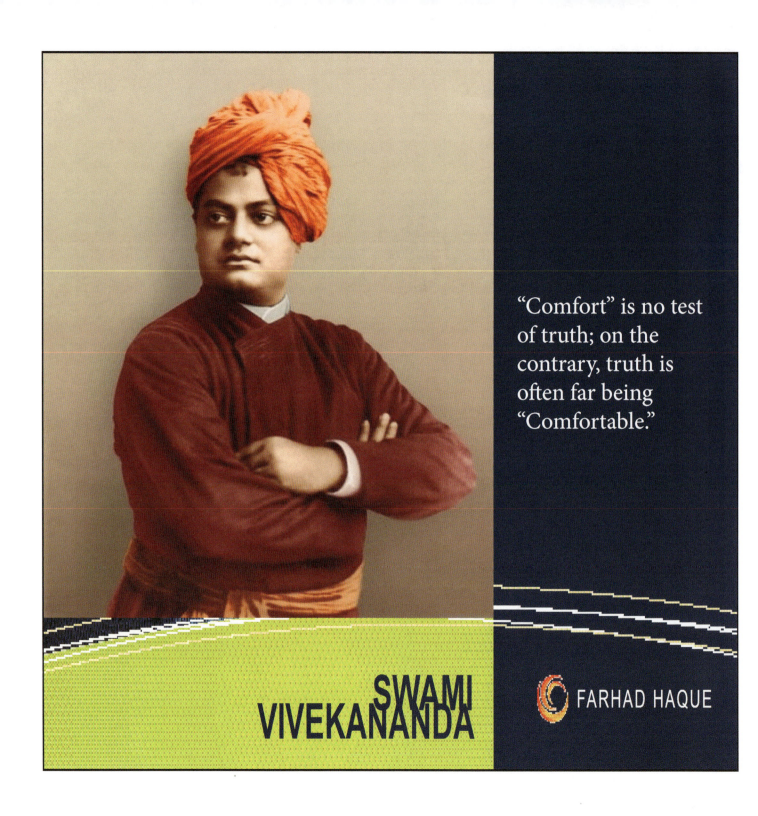

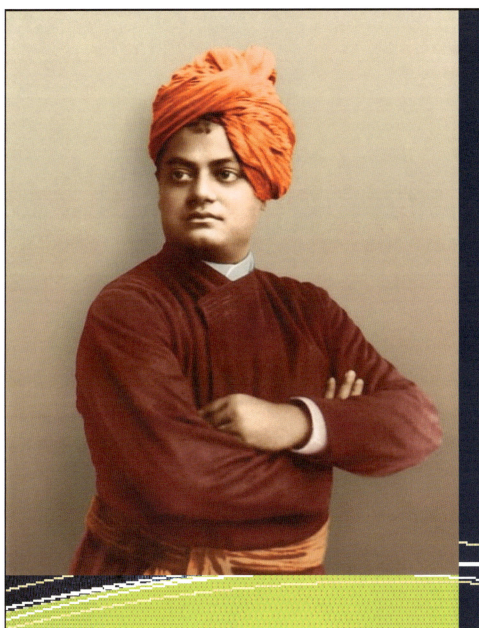

"As body, mind, or soul, you are a dream; you really are Being.Consciousness, Bliss (satchidananda). You are the God of this universe. As long as we believe ourselves to be even the least different from God, fear remains with us; but when we know ourselves to be the One, fear goes; of what can we be afraid?

SWAMI VIVEKANANDA

 FARHAD HAQUE

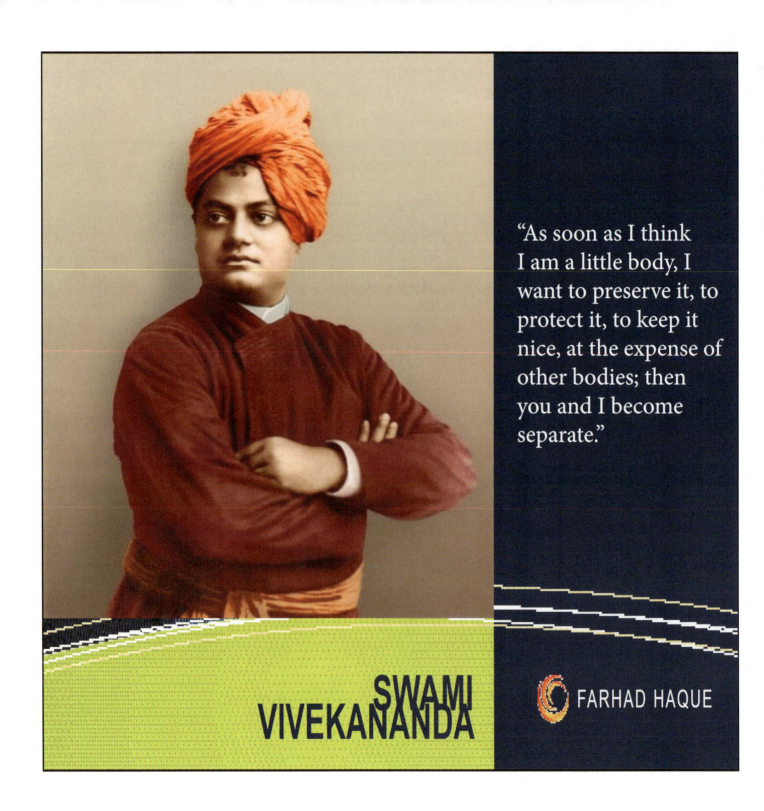

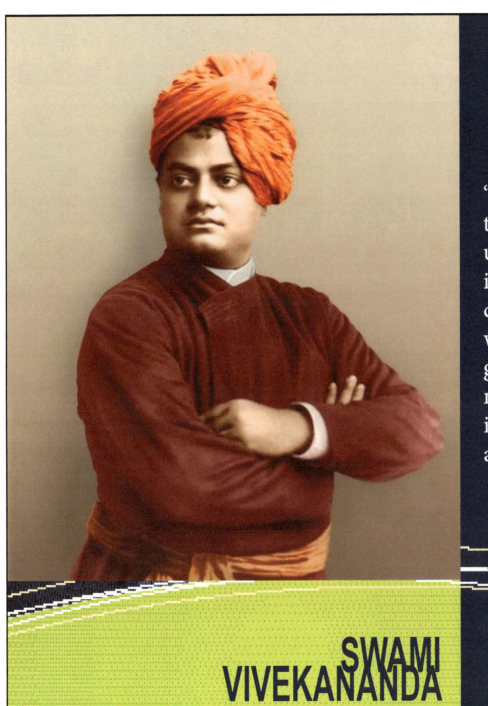

"As soon as you know the voice and understand what it is, the whole scene changes. The same world which was the ghasty battlefield of maya is now changed into something good and beautiful."

SWAMI VIVEKANANDA

 FARHAD HAQUE

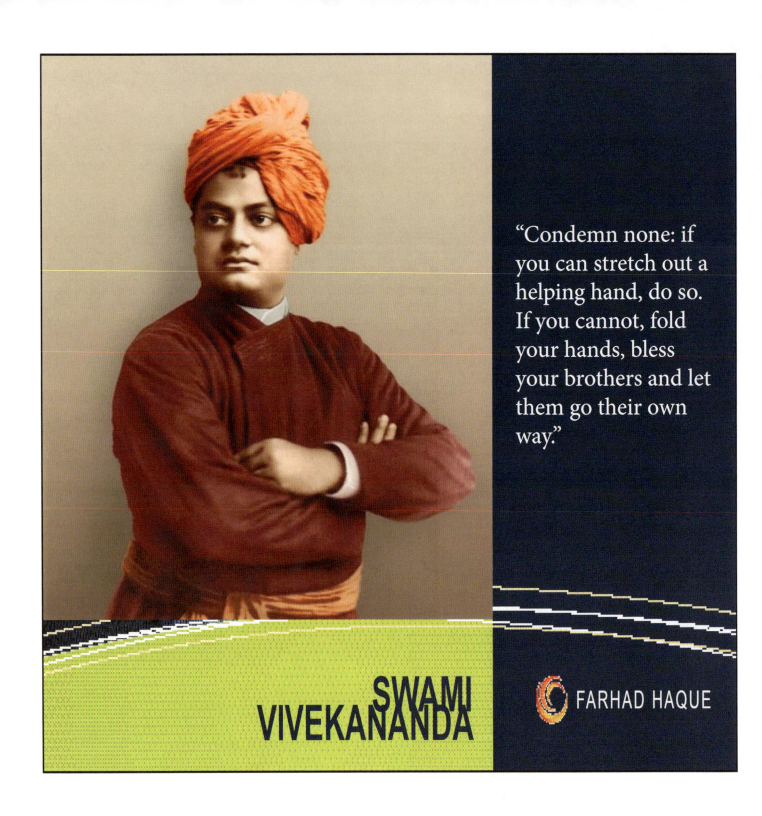

"Each work has to pass through these stages-ridicule, opposition, and then acceptance. Those who think ahead of their time are sure to be misunderstood."

SWAMI VIVEKANANDA

FARHAD HAQUE

"As long as we believe ourselves to be even the least different from God, fear remains with us, but when we know ourselves to be the One, fear goes; of what can we be afraid?"

SWAMI VIVEKANANDA

 FARHAD HAQUE

"Your atman is the support of the universe-whose support do you stand in need of? Wait with patience and love and strength. If helpers are not ready, they will come in time. Why should we be in a hurry? The real working force of all great work is in its almost unperceived beginnings."

SWAMI VIVEKANANDA

 FARHAD HAQUE

"Learning and wisdom are supperfluities, the surface glitter merely, but it is the heart that is the seat of all power. It is not in the brain but in the heart that the Atman, possessed of knowledge, power, and activity, has its seat."

SWAMI VIVEKANANDA

 FARHAD HAQUE

"Our duty is to encourage every one in his struggle to live up to his own highest idea, and strive at the same time to make the ideal as near as possible to the Truth."

SWAMI VIVEKANANDA

 FARHAD HAQUE

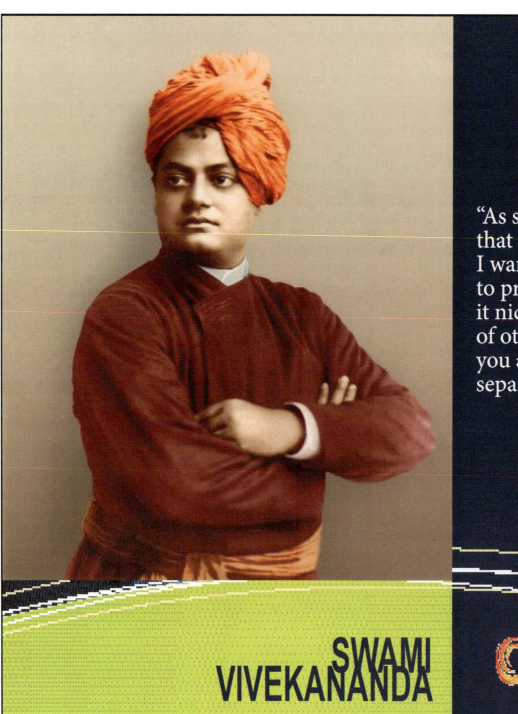

"As soon as I think that I am a little body, I want to preserve it, to protect it, to keep it nice, at the expense of other bodies; then you and I become separate."

SWAMI VIVEKANANDA

 FARHAD HAQUE

"I fervently wish no misery ever came near anyone; yet it is that alone that gives us an insight into the depths of our lives, does it not? In our moments of anguish, gates barred forever seem to open and let in many a flood of light."

SWAMI VIVEKANANDA

 FARHAD HAQUE

Reference

Virtual Maze.(2013).Swami Vivekananda(Version 1.1)[Mobile application software]. Retrieved from http://itunes.apple.com/

Made in the USA
Lexington, KY
29 May 2014